The world inside Paris

Experience you will never recover from

Nicole Guidian

Table of Contents

Introduction

It was a cold, misty morning in Paris. The streets were deserted, except for a small figure walking down the cobbled street.

It was a young woman, with a suitcase in one hand and a map in the other.

She was a stranger in a strange land, but something about the city made her feel at home.

As she walked, she could feel the energy in the city, the electricity in the air. She could feel the history and culture of the city, and she felt a connection to it.

She had only been in Paris for a few days, but it felt like she had been here her whole life.

This was a city that had seen a lot of pain and sorrow, but it had also seen a lot of joy and beauty.

She felt a deep sense of pride as she walked through the streets, and she knew that she would be back soon.

Paris was her home now, and it always would be.

The history of Paris

Paris is the capital, central and biggest city of France. It is located on the River Seine in the north of the country.

It is one of the most visited cities in the world and has been a major center of culture and industry since the Middle Ages.

The history of Paris dates back to around 3200 BC when a Celtic tribe called the Parisii settled on the banks of the Seine River.

Roman occupation between 52 BC and the 5th century AD left a lasting impression on the city. During this period, the city was known as Lutetia and was the capital of the province of Gaul.

In the Middle Ages, Paris became an important religious center and a hub of learning, art, and culture.

It was during this time that the Notre Dame Cathedral was built, and the Louvre Palace was established.

During the Renaissance, Paris was transformed into a major cultural center, with the building of the Paris Opera House, the first public library, and the first public zoo.

In the 18th century, Paris was the capital of the French Revolution, with the storming of the Bastille in 1789 marking the beginning of the revolution.

Napoleon Bonaparte declared himself Emperor of France in 1804, and Paris became.

The culture of Paris

Paris is a large and diverse city, with a culture that has been shaped by centuries of immigration, art, and history.

The city is known for its world-famous landmarks, such as the Eiffel Tower and the Louvre, as well as its vibrant nightlife and cafe culture.

The people of Paris are also a diverse and eclectic mix of cultures, from the traditional French to immigrants from around the world.

This is reflected in the city's food, music, art, and literature. Paris is renowned for its fine cuisine, which includes classic French dishes like steak frites, bouillabaisse, and ratatouille.

The city is also home to a vibrant nightlife scene with a variety of pubs, bars, and nightclubs.

The city is also known for its art and architecture. Paris is home to many iconic landmarks, such as the Eiffel Tower, the Notre-Dame Cathedral, and the Arc de Triomphe.

The city is also home to numerous museums, galleries, and theatres, which showcase some of the world's greatest art and performances.

Paris is a vibrant and cosmopolitan city, with a culture that is constantly evolving.

The people of Paris

The people of Paris are the living embodiment of the city's culture, spirit, and history.

They are a diverse mix of native Parisians, immigrants, and expats who come from all walks of life.

They can be found in the bustling streets and cafes of the city, working, playing, and embracing life to the fullest.

Parisians are typically known for their sophistication and refinement, but they are also welcoming and friendly to tourists and newcomers alike.

Whether they are in the city for work, study or simply to explore, Parisians are eager to share their knowledge and experiences with visitors.

The people of Paris are highly educated and well-informed. With a strong sense of history, Parisians take great pride in their city and its achievements.

They are passionate about their culture, art, music, and cuisine, and are always eager to share their knowledge with others.

The people of Paris work hard to keep the city vibrant and alive. From small business owners to entrepreneurs, the city's inhabitants are the lifeblood of the city.

They work together to ensure the city remains a great place to live and work, and that its legacy is preserved for generations to come.

Parisians are also passionate about the environment.

The Attractions of Paris

There are many attractions in Paris that can appeal to tourists. Some of the most popular attractions are the Eiffel Tower, the Louvre Museum, and Notre Dame Cathedral.

These attractions are all very famous and draw in large crowds of tourists every year.

The Eiffel Tower is probably the most famous attraction in Paris. It is a massive tower that was built in 1889 and is over 300 meters tall.

It is one of the most popular and attractive tourist destinations in the world.

The Louvre Museum is another very famous attraction in Paris. It is the largest art museum in the world and contains over

380,000 pieces of art. It is a must-see place for any art lover.

Notre Dame Cathedral is another popular tourist attraction in Paris. It is a beautiful cathedral that was built in the 12th century. It is a must-see place for any history lover.

Paris Food

Paris is a food lover's paradise. There are so many amazing restaurants to choose from, each with their own unique style and menu.

You can find everything from classic French dishes to exotic international cuisine.

No matter what you're in the mood for, you can find something to satisfy your cravings in Paris.

The city is famous for its delicious pastries and cheese, so make sure to indulge in some of both during your stay.

There are also plenty of street vendors selling snacks like crepes and falafel, so you can enjoy a quick and tasty meal on the go.

And of course, no visit to Paris would be complete without a cup of coffee from one of the many charming cafes.

So if you're looking for a foodie adventure, Paris is the place to be. With so many amazing restaurants and cafes to explore, you're sure to find something to your taste. Bon appétit!

Nightlife in Paris

Paris is known for its vibrant nightlife, offering something for everyone. From traditional cabarets and jazz clubs to trendy pubs and underground clubs, the City of Lights truly comes alive at night.

The Champs-Élysées is a great place to start a night out in Paris. This iconic street is lined with bars, clubs, and cafes, making it perfect for an evening stroll.

The area is also home to some of the city's most famous cabarets, including the legendary Moulin Rouge. If you're looking for a pub or bar, head to the Latin Quarter.

This area is home to some of Paris's best pubs, where you can enjoy a pint of beer and some traditional French snacks.

Many of the pubs also offer live music, so you can enjoy a night of dancing as well. If you're looking for something a bit different, the Marais district is the place to be.

Here you can find trendy clubs, lounges, and bars, many of which have a unique atmosphere.

The Marais is also home to the city's thriving LGBT scene, with several gay bars located in the area.

No matter what type of nightlife you're looking for, you're sure to find something in Paris.
From traditional cabarets to trendy clubs, the City of Lights has something for everyone.

Shopping in Paris

Shopping in Paris is an experience like no other. From high-end designer stores to vintage boutiques, Paris has it all.

Whether you're looking for the latest fashion trends, souvenirs or antiques, you'll find something to suit your taste.

High-end shopping can be found on the famous Champs-Élysées.
Here, luxury stores such as Louis Vuitton, Dior, Prada, and Hermès line the streets alongside more affordable stores such as H&M and Zara.

Department stores such as Galeries Lafayette, Printemps, and Le Bon Marché offer a variety of goods in one place.

If you're looking for something more unique, head to one of the many vintage boutiques located around the city.

The Marais district is particularly well known for its vintage stores, with a wide range of clothes, accessories, and furniture from a variety of eras.

For souvenirs, the market stalls of the Place de la Madeleine are the perfect place to pick up some traditional French souvenirs.

Here you will find a variety of items such as postcards, magnets, and keychains.

Paris is also home to a wide selection of food markets, such as the Marché des Enfants Rouges and the Marché d'Aligre.

Here, you can buy fresh fruits, vegetables, and cheeses, as well as local delicacies such as foie gras and escargots.

Shopping in Paris is an unforgettable experience, offering something for everyone. Whether you're looking for luxury, vintage, or souvenirs, you're sure to find something special.

Why Paris

There are many reasons why Paris is a popular tourist destination.

Some reasons include its rich history, beautiful architecture, and delicious food.

Paris is also a city that is full of life, with plenty of things to do and see.
Whether you are a history buff, an architecture enthusiast, or just looking for a good
eatery, Paris has something for everyone.

Paris is also a very walkable city, making it easy to get around.

You can explore the city's narrow streets, charming squares, and impressive architecture without having to worry about getting lost.

And, of course, no visit to Paris is complete without a visit to the Eiffel Tower.

So if you're looking for a city that has it all, Paris is a great choice.

Rules and regulations in Paris

In Paris, there are a number of rules and regulations that must be followed. Some of these include:

-You must be 18 years or older to purchase alcoholic drinks
-It is illegal to drink in public
-It is illegal to smoke in public
-It is illegal to sell cigarettes to young people
-You must have a valid ID to purchase cigarettes
-Do not drive under the influence of alcohol or drugs
-It is illegal to run a red light.
-It is illegal to eat or drink on the Metro
-It is illegal to litter
-It is illegal to urinate in public
-It is illegal to disturb the peace
-It is illegal to carry a weapon without a permit

-It is illegal to take pictures of police officers or military personnel
-It is illegal to post graffiti
-Do not wear a mask in public
-It is illegal to hitchhike

Conclusion

Paris is a city like no other. From the iconic Eiffel Tower to the winding streets of the Latin Quarter, it is a city filled with beauty, history, culture, and romance.

No matter how many times you visit, there is always something new to discover in the City of Light. Paris is an amazing destination that will leave you with a lifetime of memories.